HORSING AROUND

FAMOUS HORSES

By Barbara M. Linde

Gareth Stevens
Publishing

Please visit our Web site, www.garethstevens.com. For a free color catalog of all our high-quality books, call toll free 1-800-542-2595 or fax 1-877-542-2596.

Library of Congress Cataloging-in-Publication Data

Linde, Barbara M.
 Famous horses / Barbara M. Linde.
     p. cm. – (Horsing around)
 Includes bibliographical references and index.
 ISBN 978-1-4339-4624-0 (pbk.)
 ISBN 978-1-4339-4625-7 (6-pack)
 ISBN 978-1-4339-4623-3 (library)
 1. Horses–Juvenile literature. 2. Famous animals–Juvenile literature. I. Title.
 SF302.L55 2011
 636.10092'9–dc22

                                          2010025938

First Edition

Published in 2011 by
Gareth Stevens Publishing
111 East 14th Street, Suite 349
New York, NY 10003

Designer: Michael J. Flynn
Editor: Therese Shea

Photo credits: (Cover, p. 1 Whittaker and Milton), p. 19 Bob Martin/Getty Images; (cover, back cover, p. 1 wooden sign), (front cover, pp. 2–4, 6, 8, 10, 12–14, 16–18, 20–24 wood background), back cover (wood background) Shutterstock.com; p. 5 Medioimages/Photodisc/Getty Images; p. 7 SuperStock/Getty Images; p. 9 Science & Society Picture Library/SSPL/Getty Images; p. 11 MPI/Archive Photos/ Getty Images; p. 13 Jerry Cooke/Sports Illustrated/Getty Images; p. 15 English School/ The Bridgeman Art Library/Getty Images; p. 17 Hulton Archive/Getty Images.

Printed in the United States of America

CPSIA compliance information: Batch #CW11GS: For further information contact Gareth Stevens, New York, New York at 1-800-542-2595.

Contents

The "Good Horse". 4

Magnolia. 6

Blind Tom. 8

Comanche 10

Man o' War 12

Black Beauty 14

Mister Ed 16

Milton. 18

Cholla the Painting Horse 20

Glossary 22

For More Information. 23

Index 24

Words in the glossary appear in **bold** type the first time they are used in the text.

The "Good Horse"

The first battle of America's fight for independence from Britain occurred on April 19, 1775. The night before, Paul Revere rode through Massachusetts warning American colonists that British soldiers were coming. Revere wouldn't have gotten far without his horse! The British captured Revere. They let him go, but gave the horse to a British soldier. Some people say Revere's horse was named Brown Beauty. Records show that Revere had borrowed a horse with this name.

Other horses have become famous for their historic roles and talents. Read on to find out their stories.

This statue of Paul Revere on a horse is found in Boston, Massachusetts.

THE MANE FACT

Paul Revere later called the horse from his midnight ride "a very good horse."

5

Magnolia

President George Washington loved horses. One of Washington's favorite horses was Magnolia. Many people thought that Magnolia was the perfect horse. Washington trained Magnolia and tried to make him into a racing horse. In 1788, Washington traded Magnolia to a friend named Light Horse Harry Lee. Washington received 5,000 acres of land in return.

Today, another horse named Magnolia lives at Washington's farm in Mount Vernon, Virginia. Visitors can see the new Magnolia and learn about the first Magnolia's life with Washington.

George Washington is shown here on a horse in front of his Mount Vernon home.

THE MANE FACT

George Washington had 21 horses at Mount Vernon when he died.

7

Blind Tom

In the mid-1800s, a railroad was built that stretched across the United States. Over 25,000 horses and mules worked on it!

One important horse was named Blind Tom. Although he couldn't see, he worked on the railroad for over 2 years. Blind Tom helped lay about 1,000 miles (1,600 km) of track. There was a **celebration** when the railroad was finished. The workers and important railroad men were there. So was Blind Tom. Newspaper reporters wrote about his work.

While the tracks of the railroad were laid, horses carried tools, supplies, and workers.

THE MANE FACT

The word "horsepower" tells how much power a machine has. This comes from the time when machines began to do work horses had done.

Comanche

In 1868, the U.S. Army bought a horse named Comanche for $90. Captain Myles Keogh rode Comanche in the Battle of the Little Bighorn in 1876. During that battle, Lieutenant Colonel George Armstrong Custer led U.S. soldiers against Native Americans. The army was **defeated**. A few days later, men found Comanche. He was the only **survivor** of the battle from the U.S. Army.

Comanche died in 1891. His body was **preserved**. You can see Comanche at the University of Kansas Museum of Natural History.

THE MANE FACT

Comanche was wounded 12 times
in different battles.

Myles Keogh and Comanche are
shown here in a photo from 1875.

11

Man o' War

There have been many great racehorses, but most people agree that Man o' War was the greatest ever. Each of his racing **strides** covered up to 28 feet (8.5 m)!

In 1919 and 1920, Man o' War won 20 out of 21 races. In the only race he lost, Man o' War was turned the wrong way as the race began. He still came in second! In another race, he won by 100 **lengths**. Man o' War made horse racing very popular in the United States.

THE MANE FACT

Many of Man o' War's children and grandchildren went on to win famous races, such as the Kentucky Derby.

Man o' War won nearly $250,000 in prizes.

In 1877, British author Anna Sewell wrote *Black Beauty*. She hoped that the book would make people treat their horses much better.

The story is told from the point of view of Black Beauty, a workhorse. He tells of people's kindness and **cruelty**. In the late 1800s, workhorses weren't treated well. Because of the book, the treatment of horses became much better.

Black Beauty is one of the most popular books ever written. It has sold over 50 million copies. It has also been made into movies and TV shows.

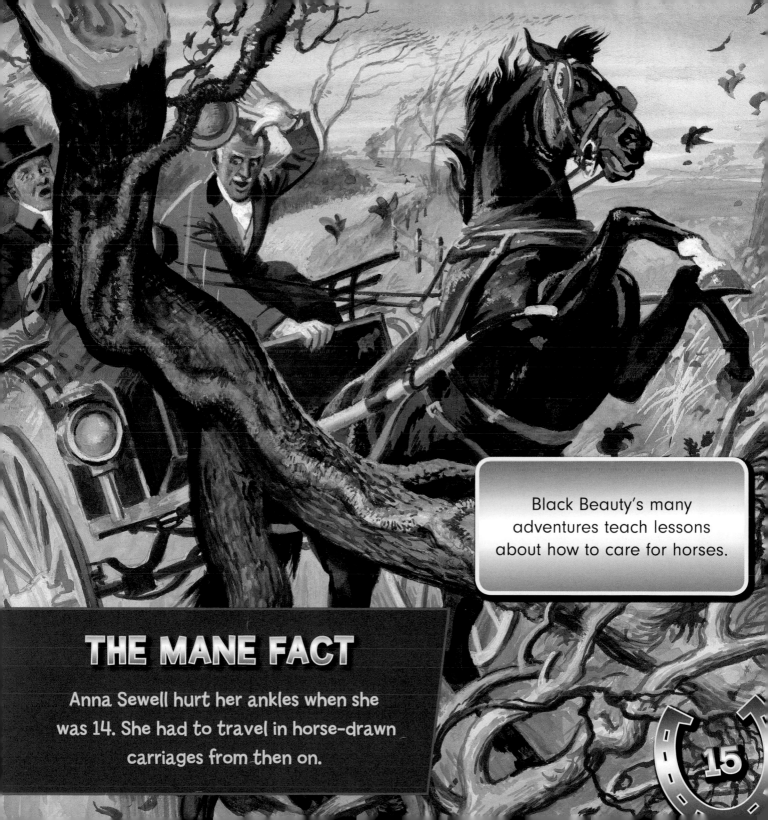

Black Beauty's many adventures teach lessons about how to care for horses.

THE MANE FACT

Anna Sewell hurt her ankles when she was 14. She had to travel in horse-drawn carriages from then on.

Mister Ed

In the early 1960s, Mister Ed was the most famous horse in the United States. His TV show, called *Mister Ed*, made it look as if he could talk. Mister Ed's trainer taught him how to move his mouth. Then, someone off camera would speak to match the movements.

In the show, Mister Ed would talk only to his owner, Wilbur. If other people were around, Mister Ed talked only when they weren't looking. Wilbur often got into trouble for the funny things that Mister Ed said!

Mister Ed poses here with actor Alan Young, who played Wilbur.

THE MANE FACT

Mister Ed's real name was Bamboo Harvester.

Milton was a gray show jumper. He was trained to jump fences, walls, and **ditches** full of water. From 1985 to 1994, Milton and rider John Whitaker **competed** in horse shows all over Europe. Milton was the first horse to earn over $1 million. He twice won an important prize called the World Cup.

Whitaker said Milton seemed human. He said the horse stuck out his tongue when he didn't want to do something! Milton was voted the best-loved horse of all time in England in 2008.

Fans sent Milton candy and birthday cards.

THE MANE FACT

Milton was sometimes called Everest Milton, Next Milton, or Henderson Milton.

19

Cholla is a horse and a famous artist! Cholla used to watch his owner, Renee Chambers, paint the fence around his pen. One day, Renee painted on a piece of paper. Then, she put a paintbrush in Cholla's mouth. He painted on the paper, too!

Renee took Cholla's paintings to art shows. She made videos to show Cholla doing his work. Many people bought his paintings. A few paintings even won prizes. Renee gives some of the paintings to **charities** to raise money for animals and sick children.

More Famous Horses of Books, TV, and Movies

Book	Horse	Rider
The Black Stallion (1941)	The Black	Alec Ramsay
My Friend Flicka (1941)	Flicka	Ken McLaughlin
TV Show	**Horse**	**Rider**
The Lone Ranger (1949–1957)	Silver	the Lone Ranger
	Scout	Tonto
The Simpsons (1989–present)	Duncan, or Furious D	Homer
	Princess	Lisa
Movie	**Horse**	**Rider**
National Velvet (1944)	Pie	Velvet Brown
Dreamer (2005)	Soñador, or Sonya	Manny

Glossary

celebration: a party in honor of a person or special event

charity: a group that helps people or animals in need

compete: to do something to win against others

cruelty: being very mean

defeat: to beat

ditch: a long, narrow path dug in the ground

length: the distance between horses in a race measured according to how long a horse is, usually about 8 feet (2.4 m)

preserve: to keep something in its original state

stride: a long step

survivor: one who stays alive after others die

For More Information

Books:

Chambers, James. *The Horse Who: Fifty Famous Horses from History.* London, England: Old Street Publishing, 2008.

Church, Lisa R. *Black Beauty: Retold from the Anna Sewell Original.* New York, NY: Sterling Publishing, 2005.

Edwards, Elwyn Hartley. *The Encyclopedia of the Horse.* London, England: Dorling Kindersley, 2008.

Web Sites:

Cholla: Horse Artist
www.artistisahorse.com
See the many paintings of Cholla, the horse artist.

Horsefun
horsefun.com
Solve horse puzzles and take quizzes on this site for young horse lovers.

Horses
www.pbs.org/wnet/nature/episodes/horses/introduction/3153/
Read about the history of horses and how they helped shape human history.

Index

Bamboo Harvester 17

Battle of the Little Bighorn 10

Black Beauty 14, 15

Black Beauty 14

Blind Tom 8

Brown Beauty 4

Chambers, Renee 20

Cholla 20

Comanche 10, 11

Custer, Lieutenant Colonel George Armstrong 10

Flicka 21

Kentucky Derby 13

Keogh, Captain Miles 10, 11

Lee, Light Horse Harry 6

Magnolia 6

Man o' War 12, 13

Massachusetts 4, 5

Milton 18, 19

Mister Ed 16, 17

Mister Ed 16

Mount Vernon, Virginia 6, 7

Revere, Paul 4, 5

Sewell, Anna 14, 15

University of Kansas Museum of Natural History 10

Washington, President George 6, 7

Whitaker, John 18

Wilbur 16, 17

World Cup 18

Young, Alan 17